Matt Manzari has survive[...] [...] more success than most indiv[...] [...] his story feels far less like an author telling you about his epic life journey and far more like a friend inviting you to more fully embrace your life journey. Do yourself a favor and read this book. You'll be profoundly inspired.

– John O'Leary
Two times #1 National Best Selling Author; Host,
Live Inspired Podcast

Matt Manzari's story is electrifying; no pun intended. It is a story about love, struggles, pain, bravery and most of all, a young man's faith in God Almighty. Anyone and everyone should read this book for a deeper insight as to what it is like to walk through the valley in discovering who we REALLY are.

– H. L. Robinson
Retired banker and Certified Stephen Covey
Leadership Trainer

Matt's story of personal perseverance, and his unique per-spective of looking at life's obstacles, is a lesson for everyone. No matter how big or how small our own issues, Matt takes the impact of his life events and makes them relatable, easy to understand, and applicable to our own challenges.

– Matt Kaplan
Vice President of Sales, Vail Resorts

I refer to my friend Matt Manzari as "Miracle Matt." Yes, because of how he's lived through events that should have easily killed him, but also because I've been with him when miracles have happened in African villages. Matt and I believe that anything is possible and that one person—YOU—can change the world. We're doing that together in reaching people with clean water—and doing it at a rate that's never been done before by any nongovernmental group—one new person reached every ten seconds. Matt's book Beyond the Scars will challenge you to find your God-given purpose and provide a guide to how you can get there. Be prepared for your plans to change—maybe quite dramatically—and experience a deeper level of satisfaction with your life.

– Greg Allgood, Ph.D.
Vice President of Water, World Vision

Matt Manzari has a powerful story that will impact readers in a big way. Get ready to have your perspective and life changed. A great book!

– Bill Yeargin
President and CEO, Correct Craft

Matt's persevering spirit and his faith in Jesus Christ would keep him from many places the world would say "he should have been." And they would lead him into new places where this champion could help others in significant *ways. This book is one of those places. It's a choice Matt made to share his story in order to inspire, challenge, and teach others how they can move past their burns, too. We all have them, you know. They just come in different forms. Thank you, Matt, for taking the time to pen your story. Thank you for not giving up and for not giving in to the pain of your burns and shattered dreams. And, thank you for being willing to help others, including me, persevere through our own difficult seasons of life.*

– Kristi Overton Johnson
Founder, Victorious Living Magazine and Prison Outreach

Matt Manzari's story is powerful and miraculous! My friend's life was not only paused; it was shaken, burned, torn, and changed to the core in an instant. If anyone had a reason to quit, it was him. God obviously had other plans for Matt's life and He is using him to inspire and give hope and purpose to so many around the world. I am proud to call him a friend!

– Paul Singer
President, Centurion & Supreme Boats

Regardless if you are facing a struggle that is catastrophic like Matt's electrocution or battling everyday struggles of marriage/parenting or the secret struggle of depression and lack of self-worth, Beyond the Scars *and Matt's life story illustrate the power of never giving up and always having hope. His story is always a fresh reset of my own perspective no matter what I'm going through.*

– Kevin Durham
Founder/Executive Director, This Is My Story

MATT MANZARI

BEYOND THE SCARS

LIFE IS DEFINED BY WHO YOU ARE, NOT YOUR CIRCUMSTANCES.

HigherLife Development Services, Inc.

P.O. Box 623307 Oviedo, Florida 32762

(407) 563-4806

www.ahigherlife.com

Printed in the United States of America.

10 9 8 7 6 5 4 3 2 1   25 26 24 23 22 21 20

Manzari, Matt

Who Are You?

Learn to Thrive in Brokenness

Paperback 978-1-951492-28-1

Ebook 978-1-954533-65-3

Connie, thank you for your love and patience through this entire process. You are an amazing listener, an amazing friend, and an amazing woman of God. Thank you for the ownership and care you gave to understanding my story. Without you I could have never gone back to the beginning to tell my story. Thank you for being my friend. I love you.

Chloe, thank you for helping build the foundation, for helping me get started in this overwhelming task.

Cassidy, thank you for loving and serving all along the way. Thank you for listening and doing the hard work of transcribing my thoughts…for listening.

CONTENTS

CHAPTER 1

MOMENTS

Today is our most precious possession.
It is our only sure possession.

— Dale Carnegie

A re you wondering where the introduction is? Well, let me start out by telling you something about myself. I do not like introductions. I know that is probably not the first fact you were expecting to learn about me, but let me explain. Most of the time when I read, I want to get to the main point of the book. I usually skim or skip the introduction then go straight to the first chapter. Sometimes this approach backfires on me, and I find myself confused when the author references something from the introduction. Then I have to stop reading and go back to figure out what the author is talking about. As I started an introduction for my book, I decided I did not want anyone to skim it and miss important information like I do, so I just decided to make the introduction the first chapter. I can break the rules in my book, right?

Most of us love making plans. We make plans to become a manager or partner at work. We make plans for our IRA, 401K, or other financial matters so we can prosper in life. Perhaps you have plans to see the Northern Lights or try surfing in Tahiti. Maybe you have plans to tell someone how you really feel. Or maybe you have plans to discover the courage to face a fear or reach a goal. We all have plans of some sort. But what happens when one moment erases all of our plans? One drastic, life-changing moment. Unexpected. Sudden. Irreversible. In one moment, our world is altered forever.

Our "world" is often constructed by experiences, relationships, and the environment we function within. As we grow and experience these things, our hopes, dreams, goals, and worldviews form. Based on that, we make plans. We make short-term plans for the present and long-term plans for our future. The basis of these plans form the life and world we hope to create for ourselves.

Think about your world and all the plans you have. Now imagine that in one moment your world and plans disappear, and you are starting life all over again. You might think, *What about my plans? What is next?* Sometimes when a drastic life change occurs, we find ourselves stuck in our own world, unable to see beyond what we have planned.

What happens when we have to look beyond? What happens when our schedule is changed permanently? All previously planned events and experiences are gone. We can no longer fulfill our role as a helpful friend, loving son, daughter, selfless spouse, or a providing parent. Now we are in a hospital, or a jail cell, and we are no longer able to go to work or drive up to our warm house after a long day. Whatever the life-changing moment that just took place—a broken relationship, a flood, or fire, a burn, spinal cord injury, a cancer diagnosis, a tumor, a verdict, a layoff, or a pay cut—our world as we know it has been taken from us.

More often than not, these moments break us, and often they break the people around us, as our world crumbles before our eyes. But these moments need not have this effect. Life is not over. Changed, yes. But it is not over.

Instead, a new world is beginning for us. We might not be able to see this new world yet, but a new life is emerging.

It is okay to laugh, cry, mourn, and miss aspects of our old life. Just like the nostalgia we feel when hearing an ice cream truck or driving down our childhood street, we can appreciate and celebrate our former world. Remembering the happy times of the past does not make our new world a bad one. It only looks bad because we do not know the plan for tomorrow, or the next day, or the next…. Our future is uncertain, and fear arises when we face uncertainty. When we do not have a plan and are not in control.

Beyond the Scars is all about how my plans kept changing as a result of tragic events, and how I adjusted to each new world I encountered. My story is full of pain—just like many others. With each life-altering moment I experienced, I knew I had to mourn my old world, yes, but I also realized I had to learn how to create a new one. With each new struggle I endured, I grew into a stronger person. And even though I have faced tough and traumatic accidents that left me forever changed, I have emerged on the other side happy and stronger. So can you.

Who are you? Are you being defined by your circumstances?

We all take a close look at ourselves and ask this question at one time or another. We ask this especially during times of life change. In times of hurt or change we can feel defeated, sad, hurt, and we allow either past or present failures and trials to start to define us. Right here, at this moment, when we feel this, is when we need to remember just who we are. The same way Simba needed to remember who he was in Disney's *The Lion King.*

Do you recall the scene where Mufasa said to Simba, "Remember who you are"?

Simba had run away from his family and his position. He was afraid everyone blamed him for his father's death, and he believed he could never go home or be who he was supposed to be.

We tend to do the same thing in our lives, don't we? Something happens and we run away, too afraid to face the fears within. Just like us, Simba could not see past his own reflection and what he felt he had become. Then, in a vision, his father tells him, "You are more than you have become."

No matter where we are in life, no matter what has happened in our lives, we were created for a greater purpose.

Wow! That is a strong statement. No matter where we are in life, no matter what has happened in our lives, we were created for a greater purpose. Despite our circumstances or struggles, we can always be more than who we have become. As we look at our own reflection in a mirror, we need to remember who we are deep inside.

The old me is gone. The new me I like; it is just etting to know him.

– Matt Manzari

My life changed forever on June 25, 2014.

My wife, Bobbye Jean, and I had no idea what kind of day we were stepping into. The morning started off as a typical day. Over morning coffee, we discussed our plans for the day. As usual, she was heading to her administrative job at a church. I was going to a dentist's appointment, then I planned to help trim trees at Bobbye Jean's work. They needed help around the church grounds, and it seemed like a fun project. We had just found out Bobbye Jean was pregnant, and we were so excited about officially sharing the news with others. Life was good, and everything seemed to be falling into place.

When I arrived at the church, Bobbye Jean reminded me to stay hydrated. High temperatures in the nineties were expected all afternoon. I remember climbing into a high-reach bucket, basically a cherry picker with wheels. I was pretty excited about the opportunity to spend the day in this piece of equipment. It felt like I was getting to hang out in a hot air balloon while using cool, manly tools, like my dad's chainsaw. My dad had bought the chainsaw I was using twenty years prior and passed it down to me. Recently I had replaced its chain and had the carburetor cleaned. I was ready to trim some trees.

I remember the metallic hum as the high reach rose from the ground. I lifted my chainsaw and started to work, listening to music over my headphones. As I cut away at the branches, I watched as they fell to the ground.

Just like a kid wanting to throw bigger and bigger rocks into the lake to see an even bigger splash each time, I instinctively watched the different ways the branches would bend, break, and pile up as they hit the ground. Time flew by. It was already after two when I decided it was time to take a break. I turned off the saw, moved the control lever forward, and watched as the tires began to slowly roll. Then…nothing. That is all I remember. I have no other memory of that day. I watched the front left tire slowly turn, and that is the last image I recall of my old life. That is the moment my life forever changed.

Here are my two grandpas, my dad with my brother, and myself standing on a massive pile of logs. The chainsaw in this picture is the exact saw I was using while trimming the trees at the church.

....

MOMENTS REFLECTION

Spend a few minutes and reflect on a moment when your life changed drastically. When the life you knew was changed forever, a time when you had to look beyond. What new life was emerging for you even though you couldn't see it in the moment? If you are facing or coping with change right now, what new life might be taking shape for you?

Consider the pieces of your old life that you miss. How did you let go of your grasp on what once was to embrace what might be?

What action or mindset change can help you not allow yesterday to prevent you from living fully today?

CHAPTER 2

FOUNDATION

I changed my thinking and it changed my life.
– Matt Manzari

My early childhood was spent in upstate New York, in the Adirondack Mountains. Most people think of New York as just skyscrapers and crowded cities, but the town I grew up in makes a small town in Colorado look huge. Life there was full of outdoor activities, which was great for an adventurous kid like me. I loved being outside. One of my favorite pastimes was building bike trails. This one trail I built started at my driveway and wove all through the woods and even our neighbors' properties. I knew every turn and jump and tree on that trail, and as I raced through it, I felt on top of the world, like a rally car driver zipping through the woods. At night, though, that same trail was terrifying, so as the sun set, I rushed back to the safety of home.

Vising my grandparents was also special. My brother and I spent time together there exploring the woods behind their house while pretending to be Davey Crocket or Indians. I remember building a lean-to with our grandpa. We would go outside there and eat lunch, pretending to be Indians who lived in the woods. Our grandpa also taught us to fish in the small stream behind his house; then he helped us clean the fish, so we could eat them that night for dinner. We were so proud. We felt like real Indians who lived off the land.

I grew up snowboarding in the wintertime, and we spent the summers on the lake skiing. If I was not on the water, I was skateboarding. I learned to water ski when I was three or four years old and was ready for a wakeboard at the age of six. Wakeboarding was fun for me because it was a lot like snowboarding. The only difference was that falling in the water did not hurt as much as falling on the ground.

I was always outside either on land or water. Many of these memories include my brother.

When I was eleven, we moved to Florida, which is known as one of the watersports capitals of the world. Many pros in the action sports world live here part-time because there are many lakes where they can train, and where snow is minimal. I was living within an hour of over 80 percent of the athletes I had looked up to my whole life. What a great place to live as a kid. I could skateboard whenever I wanted, but with all the water around I soon found myself wakeboarding a lot more. I also started doing a sport called wakeskating, where I felt right at home. It is like wakeboarding without bindings, so you are actually skateboarding on the water. How amazing is that? My friends and I enjoyed wakeskating and the challenge it brought. It was not long before my passion grew for the sport and my dream of becoming a professional materialized.

Wakeskating became my passion.

How often have you heard the statement, "You can do anything you set your mind to"? Ponder this statement for a moment. Do you really believe you can do anything? It is so easy to hear sayings like this and brush them off. Just like commercials, we may see on television or social media about third world kids dying because they do not have clean water. We watch these commercials or read the posts and think about how sad their situation is. Do we do anything? Most of us do not do anything. The next commercial comes on or the next post captures our attention and our thoughts have shifted. We have changed the channel. Just like that, we have forgotten about the kids. We often hear tragic stories then quickly move back into the routine of our lives. But what would happen if we took a different approach? What if we truly and honestly listened to the counsel that we could, in fact, succeed at anything we put our mind to?

The reality is, by the time you have read through this page, one child from that commercial or post we ignored has died from not having clean drinking water. One child under the age of five dies every two minutes. How crazy is that? Does it stir emotion in you? We can apply this analogy to our lives and how we respond to a challenge.

The reality is that you CAN do anything you set your mind to. Does reading this stir emotion in you? Or do you ignore it and move on to something else? Maybe you choose something easier, something that you know you can accomplish without much effort. Or do you take it to heart and make the decision to tackle your dream? Do you make a goal list and find friends to help hold you accountable? For me, I had heard encouraging phrases like this my entire life and more often than not I brushed them off. They never really sunk in until my dad told me a story about a man named Roger.

Roger Banister is a man who changed an entire industry and sport. Roger was a track athlete back in the 1950s. In those days, the fastest mile time for running was four minutes or more. It was a known fact by runners, coaches, and experts that nobody could do it in under four minutes. They did not believe our bodies would ever be able to perform at that level. Roger made the decision to think differently. He kept pushing the limits until he broke the mental barrier that was holding himself and others back. In May of 1954, Roger Banister broke the four-minute mark by one second. He ran a sub-four-minute mile! He made the impossible possible by just pushing the limit. Just six years later, thirty more people beat the record. Today, hundreds have surpassed it. So, what changed? One second changed everyone's mindset. Because Banister proved it could be done, they decided they could do it, too. They tore down the mental barrier and trained their physical bodies to accomplish the feat.

No matter where we are in life, no matter what has happened in our lives, we were created for a greater purpose.

We are often so busy comparing ourselves to everyone else, that we miss our biggest competitor. The person staring back at us when we look in the mirror is usually the only one holding us back. As a fourteen-year-old kid, I realized that I did not have to be an average kid who just loved a sport. I wanted to be that person who pushed the limits of what was possible and help shape a sport. I began trying new tricks that no one else was doing. With determination and a never-give-up attitude, I saw myself completing each trick until I succeeded. It took a true belief that the goal had already been accomplished, even though it had not. Just like Roger Banister, I broke the mental barrier that was preventing me from succeeding.

Before I knew it, I got a call from a small company in Oregon called Nike. My riding had caught their attention and they offered me the first wake contract for their new action sports sector called Nike 6.0. With that contract signed, I was traveling the world doing what I loved at the young age of fifteen! I was not any better than any other person in the

action sports world. I had just chosen to think differently. I decided to expect more from myself than anyone else
ever would. I changed my thinking and it changed my life.
This was the beginning of my pro status in wakeskating and
where I found my identity and began to make plans for the
rest of my life. My life foundation was laid.

I was proud of my Nike sponsorship.

....

FOUNDATION REFLECTION

What dreams and skills do you have that you have not yet fully developed or used to help someone else? Is there something you have always wanted to do but have considered it impractical or just too hard?

What is that thing you have always wanted to do?

Remember that you can do anything you set your mind to. Let these words stir you, and this time, do not ignore the emotion. Write down three personal goals in a notebook or planner, and then start formulating a plan to reach these goals. Make sure to include deadlines for each milestone and a target completion date. If your goal is to pursue a higher degree, start researching schools that offer your chosen field of study, research carefully, and gather all the information needed to apply. Whatever your three goals are, create a written plan for each with actionable steps. If your goal is to spend more time with family, plan family time and activities in your calendar, and make sure to follow through. Next share your goals and plans with an accountability partner—a family member, a friend, or a coach. This person is there to keep you motivated, on task, and moving toward success. Like Roger Banister, don't allow the voices, whether they are internal or external, prevent you from working to accomplish your goals.

CHAPTER 3

CROSSROADS

One of the hardest decisions you will ever face in life is choosing whether to walk away or try harder.

– Unknown

We talked about making plans in chapter one and how these plans can change at any given moment. At age fifteen, I pretty much had my entire life planned out. While I knew my knees would not last forever as a professional athlete, I had a foot in the door with some pretty big brands. One day, when I did stop riding competitively, I figured I would switch to a team management position or work for one of the companies that had sponsored me. One way or another, I was certain my career would always be in the sports world. A couple of years into my career, though, things started changing. I found myself at a crossroads of some sort. I could not see past my plans, but I began to notice my at-first-hoped-for-then-envisioned-life that was within my grasp was self-centered. My life was all about me. And there, with my dreams coming true, I realized my vision would not bring me fulfillment. The adventure was losing its satisfaction. In magazines and other communications, articles written about me said I cared about others and I liked to help people, which sounded great. My daily actions, however, didn't reflect my words. My heart and mind were traveling in different directions; I felt divided. Where was I to find God and my family, friends, and relationships in my self-centered world? Something had to change. A shift needed to happen.

Have you ever had a plan that you thought, if achieved, would bring you fulfilment? Maybe it was a relationship. Maybe it was a job you believed would make you happy and fulfilled. Perhaps it was just the only thing you ever wanted, but it ultimately left you miserable and broken. Now you are sitting at your desk reading this, wondering what is next. We often think we know best, but our plans can leave us emptier and more confused than we felt before we made them.

I do not know what your biggest plan for your life might be, but mine had pretty much come true. I was getting paid to compete in my favorite sport and travel the world with my friends. I always believed my goals would make me happy. If I could only win this contest. If I could only get on the cover of this magazine. Or if I could acquire that next endorsement from a high-level brand, I would be happy. What I found out was that as my biggest dreams came true, it was never enough. It was fun and made me happy for a time, but it was short-lived. I was striving for something to fill a void and was never able to truly fill it.

Being at the top was amazing to experience. But I knew there was more to life.

I have studied psychology pretty extensively. One of the most inspiring insights I experienced was getting the opportunity to read people's last words. It was amazing to discover that at the end of people's lives all that mattered were relational regrets. I read a few hundred of them…the teacher I was working with had read thousands. He told me that never once had he read one that had anything to do with wishing somebody had worked more or been more successful or had more material wealth.

This is a profound observation and reflection.

We spend our lives planning how to make ourselves happy by trying to get a foot ahead of everybody else, by trying to be successful and reach certain statuses. But in the end, what really matters is people—especially the ones we care about. What matters is our how we focus and pour into our relationships. My conclusion in all of this is that if our goals only include ourselves, we are going to be empty, lonely, and miserable. We will lack the fulfillment we seek to attain.

I experienced this unfulfillment firsthand by spending many years trying to fill a cup that I could never fill. The successes were never enough. Weighing heavily on my heart was the stark reality that I needed to make a life change. I kept feeling like there was something more I was supposed to do. While I did not know what the "more" was, I did know that I was completely empty. I knew God was calling me to do something different. I knew the next step had to be bigger than me. It had to be a place where I put others first. For months I felt this heart tug, but I was hesitant to completely change my life because I was full of fear. This change would require commitment from me, a commitment that might alter my livelihood as well as my identity. And my career was going so well. How could I give that up? Did I really want to give it up?

One day, it all came to a head. I woke up and immediately felt that same weight of emptiness on my shoulders again. The one I had been trying to ignore. Something had to give, and that day, desperately needing clarification, I cried out to God. At that crossroad in my life, I needed a clear answer as to which way to go. For two long months, I had not shared my struggle with anyone.

An hour after asking God for clarification and direction, I was heading to Orlando for a photoshoot and got a call from one of my friends in California. This friend of mine is a pretty extreme guy. He was certainly not the person I expected God to use in my life. As we were talking, he randomly told me that he knew from the day he met me that I would go on to serve people, live out the plan that God had for me, and would no longer be in the industry like I was. This was a clear sign and I immediately knew it was God.

The next few months were a whirlwind. Suddenly, I was enrolled at a university in Tennessee and getting ready for my first semester, which was only a few months away. I had to make the dreaded phone calls to my team managers to let them know my decision to go to college. I was fully expecting to be fired when I called, but instead I was pleasantly surprised at their responses. They paid for me to produce certain results, and if I could continue ranking as a top athlete, they did not see a need to make any changes to my contract.

With that settled, I went off to school, eager and excited to begin a new chapter. I went from traveling the world on my own as an adult to living in a basement, abiding by an eleven o'clock curfew, and attending a conservative university. The shift was much harder than I had anticipated. My classes were more challenging than I had ever imagined. Keeping my grades up was a real struggle. I felt as though everyone else "got it" easily and I had to work twice as hard. Quickly it became apparent that my goofing off in high school while focusing on my sports career had hindered my college readiness.

College was a completely different challenge.

Maybe you are experiencing something similar in your life now. I was definitely feeling overwhelmed and lost. The truth is, sometimes we get pushed beyond our limits. We find the courage to take that chance and then things become tough. What do we do then? Do we start questioning our decision? My life was full of crossroads, and I had to make the decision to trust in the truth I knew. I had to continue the course I had chosen, even though it was going to be challenging.

---

*Let me both encourage and assure
you that there is a way through any
problems you face.*

Let me encourage you to do the same. Crossroads are hard for everyone. There will be times when you will get scared, especially when you cannot see the finish line anywhere in sight. Maybe you are up to your neck in bills and debt and you feel like you will never be able to dig yourself out. Maybe your relationship is in such a bad place that a divorce or a breakup seems like the only option. Maybe you are so depressed about the place you are at in life that you cannot see a way to get to where you would like to be. It may require too many changes on your end. Maybe you are lacking the encouragement and support of others and you just do not know where to begin. Let me both encourage and assure you that there is a way through any problems you face. It is as simple as taking one step at a time and trusting the truth that there is a course of action that can and will bring you to freedom. Remember, you are more than your circumstances.

....

CROSSROADS REFLECTION

Have you ever had a plan that you thought, if achieved, would bring you fulfillment, only to find it left you empty? In that place of unfulfillment, did you change your plans and start in a new direction, one more heart-centric? If so, did you run into roadblocks and difficulties? How did you handle them?

If you are at a crossroad right now, let me assure you that while change might be difficult, it is possible to either start over or make changes right where you are that allows peace to enter into your life. I encourage you to reflect on what exactly steals your peace and satisfaction and then make adjustments to your life or schedule to reclaim it.

CHAPTER 4

CLARITY

For God is not the author of confusion, but of peace….
– 1 Corinthians 14:33, KJV

So there I was, dropped into this foreign place where they speak a different language, this place called college. I went from an industry where I knew the key players to engulfed in a world of school, where I did not know anybody. In my wakeskating career, I had all the connections necessary and knew what I needed to do to be successful. College was a whole new playing field. Everywhere I looked was blurry. The only constant I had in my life was an amazing girl I had started dating shortly before leaving for Tennessee.

This is Bobbye Jean and I while we were dating.

Of course, this wonderful young lady became my wife, Bobbye Jean. We had known each other since we were fourteen, but had only started dating shortly before I left for college. Bobbye Jean was super surprised when I asked her out. She did not think I liked her in that way, when in fact I was completely crazy about her from the beginning. Bobbye Jean or "Bob" as she was called just felt like one of the guys in the group. It did not take long—as a matter of fact, only three months into dating—when I knew she was the one.

I know three months is not very long, but I had complete clarity about it.

The next step was asking her parents for her hand in marriage. I remember that day. I was so excited sitting across the table from Bobbye's parents. After I asked them, all I remember wondering is why their jaws were on the breakfast table. Why were they not jumping up and down with excitement? Surely, it was not because we were so young or that we had only been dating for three months? Maybe it was the fact that I was her first boyfriend?

Honestly, they were only behaving as any other parent would. As a parent myself, I am always concerned about the future of my children. I do not want them to make the same mistakes I did or fail in any way. I left breakfast knowing that Bobbye Jean's parents loved me and cared for me. I knew they were excited about our future but were hesitant about telling two eighteen-year-olds that it was time to get married. I was a little disappointed when I called my dad to tell him about my morning. He assured me it would be okay. It was maybe an hour after breakfast that both Bobbye Jean's parents texted me. The message simply said, "Yes." I believe my dad may have shared his own experience of getting married young with Bobbye Jean's parents. However it happened, I was thankful for the answer.

Next, it was time to plan the perfect proposal. Bobbye Jean was a 4.0 student and one of the smartest people I knew, but her hardest subject was probably geography. She still struggles with it today. I was really hoping to play that to my advantage. I had it all worked out. I would be home for Thanksgiving break, and I would ask her to travel part of the way back to school with me. We would stop in Asheville, North Carolina, to meet my aunt and uncle. Then I would take her to Atlanta, Georgia, where she could jump on a flight back to Florida and I would head on to Tennessee. Okay, those of you who know geography are probably thinking this is a giant "Z" on a map. It was, but I was hoping she would not notice. I had to get her to Asheville.

Bobbye Jean loves Christmas lights and decorated houses. So what better place to propose than the biggest house in the country? The Biltmore is a huge estate in North Carolina. It has an annual Christmas display and candlelight tours that start right after Thanksgiving. Thank goodness she was not on to me. I was able to get her to the Biltmore under the disguise of wanting to show her the Christmas decorations and have a nice dinner. After going on the candlelight tour and before our dinner reservations, we went out on a bridge that overlooked the entire property. Walking up the steps, I nervously made surface-level conversation about the architecture of the steps and how they are kind of a funny height.

When we got to the top of the bridge, it was finally time. I got on one knee and I asked her to be my wife. She smiled ear to ear, put her hands over her face, and asked, "Do our parents know?" Bobbye Jean remembers this a little differently and swears that "yes" was the first word that came out of her mouth. For me, it felt like an eternity waiting on her answer. Either way, it turned out perfect. I pulled it off. Our plan was to wait four years after we both graduated college. Yet, after two years the distance was too much to manage and we decided to get married.

I pulled it off!

We were so excited to finally be together, and we had a clear picture of the direction our life was going. We had an awesome life and two years went by really quickly. Graduation was approaching quickly, and all my contracts were up with my sponsors. I was looking forward to the future. I had been sending out resumes and was willing to accept God's plan, wherever it took me.

We were so excited to finally be together, and we had a clear picture of the direction our life was going.

In the meantime, I came up with a great plan. We would move back to Florida to be near family and friends while I waited for a job opportunity to arise. Realizing the pro-wakeskate tour would be starting in Florida around the same time, I decided to enter the contest. It would be a great way to earn some extra money. We knew it would take two trips to move everything down, so we made our plans to travel down with one load before the contest. After the contest, we could go back to Tennessee for my finals, graduation, and the last load of our belongings. In my mind, it was a great plan especially when everything started to fall into place. As time got closer, I even received a phone call about a job opportunity based in Florida. All the doors appeared to be opening. We finally had clarity. What could possibly go wrong?

We arrived in Florida with our first load just before the wakeskate competition. I was excited to be back on the water again. The contest was on April 20, 2012, and I was the first rider off the dock. As I stood on the dock, I felt very comfortable and confident. I had ridden this lake many times and knew how many tricks I could do before getting to the narrow pass we had to enter. I was having a great run. The boat was moving about twenty-three miles an hour, but my body was jumping over the wakes that the boat was producing and this increased my speed to well over thirty miles an hour. At this heightened speed, I went in to do my last jump before the canal and somehow misjudged the distance. I knew my limits and calculated my risks, or so I thought. The next thing I knew I was surrounded by doctors telling me not to move.

....

CLARITY REFLECTION

Change is never easy. When have you been in a new environment? Perhaps you began a new career, and were unsure of your ability to succeed, and even more unsure of your decision to even begin this road. How did you handle the uncertainty? Perhaps you are a seasoned professional and have become accustomed to achieving the same level of success or performance each and every day. Until that one day....

Now, while most people have not experienced a devastating professional wakeskating accident, everyone has faced a life-altering situation or event, a job loss, an illness, a breakup, the loss of a loved one.... What was this life-altering situation or event for you? Is there a moment in your life when you just could not fulfill a goal or expectation? What lessons did you learn from the experience?

CHAPTER 5

BROKENNESS

I had never had a broken bone before this accident.

– Matt Manzari

L ater I was informed that I had crashed into the shoreline, which was full of rocks, cinderblock, and concrete with rebar from sidewalks. It was a very narrow passage, and to avoid erosion on the shoreline as boats went by, construction debris was dumped there. Upon impact, I cracked my skull in sixteen places. One of the descriptions from a doctor that examined my nasal passage compared it to a box of Rice Krispies. The bones were just shattered. My hand was crushed, rebar went through my leg, my tailbone was broken, and my jaw was broken. It took multiple screws and plates to rebuild my face. Doctors were amazed that I survived the head trauma alone. The area all around my temple was shattered, along with my eye socket. It should be noted that this temple area is a junction. It is where the skull bones come together. This causes a weak area with no solid bones behind it. There is also an artery that runs behind it. So a blow half as hard as I had should have taken my life.

The result of landing on those rocks.

I was grateful to be alive, but my whole world was flipped upside down. Going into the competition, I had so many plans, and in one moment everything just stopped. Not long before the competition, I became involved with a nonprofit that allowed me to come alongside athletes to help them tell their faith stories through film. That summer I planned to travel the country to show these stories and tell mine to kids everywhere. How was I going to do all I had committed to do? I was helpless.

So many details needed to be worked out. I still had finals to take at school. I even had a mission trip to go on that would give me the field credits I needed to graduate. With our upcoming move back to Florida, I still had to figure out our living arrangements. How was I going to take care of my wife? We were at a standstill, with a million things still left to happen.

This is how life goes though, right? Is it not? It has a funny way of interrupting our plans.

_____

*I was not ungrateful to be alive; I was
actually excited and thankful to be alive.*

_____

I used to believe that I relied on my faith pretty heavily, but at that moment I realized I had been relying on myself much more. It was my job to fix this horrible situation. In my mind, finding the solutions was all on my shoulders. How was I going to accomplish anything while lying in this hospital bed? I was not ungrateful to be alive; I was actually excited and thankful to be alive. With my life being such a mess, I saw no way that I could help myself out of this brokenness. I had to learn how to walk again using a walker, and with my jaw being rebuilt, I could not even open my mouth wide enough to slide a toothbrush between my teeth. I could not eat solid food for months. How was I going to fix these situations? How was I going to take the next step when I could not even walk without a walker?

Soon enough, all the struggles began to sort themselves out. My friend from school stepped in and went on the mission trip in my place. The university worked with me so I could still graduate on time. My parents were gracious enough to open their home to us. While Bobbye Jean worked, my parents took care of me until she got home.

Eight months later, I had fully recovered physically, but I was emotionally and spiritually changed forever. Everything I had worried about had worked out so far! I remember looking at the bills we needed to pay over the next few weeks and our bank account balance and realizing we did not have enough money to cover them all. I knew my parents would lend us money if we asked, but they had already done so much for us, and we did not want to ask. I wanted to start pulling my own weight as the head of my household. I wanted to provide for my family, and I was healthy enough to start working. I went out looking for a job and got a job that very same day allowing Bobbye and I to be able to take care of our bills. I was learning how to thrive during the interruption of my plans.

Are you in a situation where you are completely overwhelmed? Have you been running scenarios through your head, but you just do not see any viable options? Maybe you are worried about bills at the end of the month. Maybe you are worried about a tough conversation you need to have that you know is going to end badly no matter which way you approach it.

That is exactly where I was when I came into this whole situation, but in hindsight, everything was taken care of. I had spent four years studying how God wanted me to treat people and trust in Him, yet living this experience showed me a very different version of Him. What I saw was a very personal and intimate God who cared for me. He was a God who put people and solutions in place as He walked with me through each of my challenges, big or small.

Think back to a difficult time in life where you faced a major struggle. Maybe you felt hopeless and broken as well. Maybe you felt that the only way to move forward would be a way that brought more brokenness and pain. Now as you read this, and you pause to think back on that moment, you can see that you are a different person. Even if the process was shorter or longer than you expected, you grew from this situation. You can now see that things worked out in ways that you could not understand at the time.

Everywhere I looked and said, "God, but what about... ?"
He would say, "I am right here."
– Matt Manzari

When I was in college I had classes with a guy named Myron. He was the kind of guy that no matter how hard of a day you were having, as soon as you saw him, you would smile ear to ear. When he saw you he would act like he was seeing a long-lost friend or the president of the United States. He would throw his arms up and wrap you in a huge bear hug. Myron was much older than me as he had decided to go back to college in his late fifties. I have never met someone so full of joy. Myron just had a personality that allowed him to be more joyful than other people. One day, in a class that Myron and I took together, we went on a retreat to the mountains. We went to this cabin to participate in exercises designed to help us learn more about who we are so we could better understand other people.

For one of the exercises, we were asked to go find a quiet place in the woods and think of pivotal situations that helped shape who we are. The situations could be a special bonding moment of a father/son fishing trip or a mother/

daughter weekend. It could have been an encouraging comment from a teacher or losing a loved one at a young age. Basically, any situation, big or small, that impacted your life. This exercise was simple. If it was a positive situation that impacted us, we were to write it on a yellow Post-it® note. If it was a negative one, we would write it on a pink Post-it® note. In the end, we were to stick all our notes on a big piece of paper so we could see all of the situations that helped shape who we are.

As I sat there and looked at my piece of paper near the end of the exercise, I felt bad because it looked like I had a big yellow piece of paper. All of the moments and events that shaped me were positive and fun. Feeling like I needed something pink, I think I put one or two things on a piece of paper that were relatively light-hearted. Something like getting grounded. I thought this was a pretty cool exercise, and I started to head back to the cabin. Just before getting there, I spotted Myron. In each hand, he had two sheets of paper that were solid pink, with only one or two yellow spots. I remember instantly choking up and feeling a pit in my stomach as my whole worldview shifted. If I were to do this exercise today, this moment would be on my paper.

I had never considered that someone so joyful could have experienced so much pain. I awkwardly greeted Myron, instantly wanting to ask him what could have been so hard and how he came through it so strong. Later, I was more in awe after sitting with him and hearing more of his story. It was a life filled with losing many loved ones close to him, about his family walking away from him, about people around him closing the door over and over, and about a long trail of many different challenges. His story gave me a whole different view of pain and hardship. Maybe the things we dread and do not see a way out of help shape our appreciation for living each day. I know I have never been the same since that day.

I learned so much through the horrible wakeskating accident and my long recovery. I was grateful to be on the other side of it. I knew I would pass the principles and lessons learned on to my kids and grandkids one day. Having a full recovery was a gift, and I did not want to take advantage of my second chance. I decided that in whatever challenges lay ahead, there would be a way through, even when I may not see it. Surely, this would be the worst I would ever have to face. Little did I know, this terrible situation was actually just preparing me for a much darker storm two years ahead.

....

BROKENNESS REFLECTION

Have your plans been interrupted unexpectedly? Of course they have. Think back to the most memorable time this occurred in your life and again consider how details worked out in the end. What did you learn from this experience of yours? How did your perspective of community shift as a result?

In your community of loved ones, whose life story has most impacted you in a positive direction? Who do you most admire for who they became despite the difficulties, the brokenness they faced? Can you find the same qualities this person possesses within yourself?

CHAPTER 6

EXPOSED

You only get one near-death experience in a lifetime, right?
– Matt Manzari

D o you recall the moment just before my life changed forever that I shared in chapter one? The left tire slowly turning? There I was, watching that tire, listening to my music. Then, all of a sudden… nothing. I do not recall anything about that day after that moment. Unfortunately, Bobbye Jean has these images stuck in her head and she likely will for the rest of her life. I was up in a metal, high-reach bucket, trimming trees. I was moving the bucket to take a water break. The bucket was sitting a pretty far distance away from the trees and power lines at this point. I am not sure how it happened, but the electricity from the powerlines jumped over to the bucket. The electricity flowed throughout the bucket and into my hands, which were holding the controls. Somewhere between twelve and twenty thousand volts of electricity flowed through my left hand to my right, traveling through the center of my chest.

When I talk about voltage and amperage, it just sounds like terms to measure numbers. Think about this for a second though. When the electric chair was used as the main method of execution for prisoners on death row, only about two thousand volts of electricity were used. The amount of electricity that ran through me was similar to being hooked up to six electric chairs at the same time. The muscle tissues in my chest, arms, wrists, and neck were immediately damaged as I was burned from the inside out. Even parts of my bones were charred. If you are wondering what that looks like, think about being in a science class in grade school. In the textbook, they have photos of the muscular system. The pictures show half of the body with skin and the other half without. This is how I looked since the skin and muscle had immediately burned away.

One of the other men helping at the church went inside to get Bobbye Jean. When she first came out, she saw me lying in the bottom of the bucket. Thinking I had passed out from heat exhaustion, Bobbye Jean ran back inside to grab help. One of the other guys there had used high reaches before, so he and others were frantically trying to lower the bucket. The controls were not responding in the way they were supposed to because the electricity had damaged them. While everyone was trying to get me down, I unknowingly started screaming and thrashing so hard that everyone thought I was going to fall over the safety rails in the bucket. At this time, they could see something besides heat exhaustion was wrong. Bobbye Jean thought maybe I had cut myself with the chainsaw.

By the time the EMTs got there, the bucket had finally started to lower back down to the ground. When they got me down low enough to see me, they all agreed that it was too horrific for my wife to see, so they held her back and would not let her come near me. Bobbye Jean remembers pushing past one lady shielding her, only to be stopped by the youth pastor of the church. They were trying to spare her but she insisted that she needed to say goodbye. When she got to me I was thrashing like crazy and screaming. She just started screaming over me telling me she loved me and that everything was going to be okay. In one sudden moment, our lives had changed forever.

He was black, charred and did not look human.
– Bobbye Jean Manzari

By this time they realized I had been electrocuted. Have you ever heard of fourth- or fifth-degree burns? I had no idea what that meant when I heard it. Fourth degree means that my muscle was destroyed and fifth degree means that the burns had reached my bones. The electricity melted most of the skin on my upper body, burned through the muscle in my chest and arms, and left my bones charred.

My left rib, sternum, and clavicle had been exposed. The electricity traveled through the headphones I was wearing, melting my phone onto my leg. It then proceeded to travel back up the headphones, exploding the buds in my ears, and then exiting my head in two places. Electricity burns from the inside out, and it is relentless. It continues moving until it finds an exit route, with no regard to the damage it causes along the way. Even the high-reach bucket's four heavy-duty construction-grade tires could not escape. Over thirty feet away from the bucket, they had melted into the concrete of the sidewalk from the electricity. How could it be that I was still alive? If I lived to recover, what would my life be like? How would I move forward with Bobbye Jean or my family?

Surely we could not get a second miracle; surely we would not be the ones who beat the odds once again.

I was falling in and out of consciousness and the ride to the hospital was brutal. While strapped to a gurney in the back of the ambulance, I was punching and yelling uncontrollably. My body was in shock and with so much pain pulsing through my body I had absolutely no control or awareness of what I was doing. In the midst of all this, Bobbye Jean was in front of an ambulance heading to the same hospital we went to for the first accident. As she sat there a second time, her mind was racing. Surely we could not get a second miracle; surely we would not be the ones who beat the odds once again. Especially after what she just saw, especially after what she was told, it did not seem there could be any chance of hope. She knew that we would never be the same again but hoped that I would remain alive and a part of her life in any capacity possible.

My ambulance driver had to make a tough decision. My accident literally happened across the street from another well-known hospital in Florida. He knew that they could not handle this level of trauma, so he made the decision to make the ten-minute drive to the only level one trauma center in Central Florida. A level one trauma center means that they have a supply of all the blood types on hand and a staff of trauma doctors and surgeons available at all times. He knew I would need this level of care if I survived the ride there. By the time we got to the hospital, the doctors were amazed that I still had a pulse. I was then immediately wheeled into the operating room. The goal at that point was just to get me stable. Every moment that I was alive from that point forward was purely miraculous.

The doctors detailed a list of my injuries to my family. It was abundantly clear to my loved ones that this was going to be a life-altering experience for all of us. From this point forward, life would never be the same. The doctors informed my family that my chance of survival was extremely low. My body would shut down; it was just a matter of time. The doctors' plan was to keep me comfortable until I passed. My family was not willing to accept the state I was in; they were terrified and scared. They were willing to plead and argue with the doctors to make sure the doctors exhausted every possible option, even if it gave them just a sliver of hope. Not only was the inside of my body physically exposed, but now I was exposed to an array of other issues and complications. My family was now exposed to the risk of losing their husband, father, son, brother, and grandson. This was going to be a long uphill battle, but we had God on our side. The waiting room became a war room for my family and friends. They gathered together for strength praying around the clock, begging God to save my life. I did not know it yet, but I was going to have to learn to thrive through this storm as well.

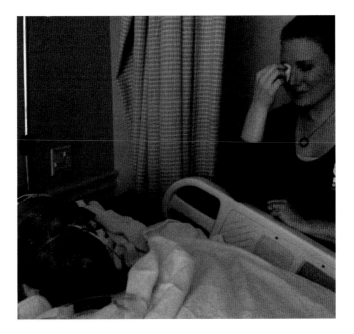

Bobbye Jean standing vigil over my bed.

Exposed Reflection

Life is not meant to be a solo game. We all need a community, a team, an army of friends, family (either biological or adopted or self-chosen). We need loved ones. Not one of us is capable of living life alone. Still, some of us find it extremely difficult to ask for help or accept assistance because doing so reveals weakness.

When have you reached the end of your own ability or capacity and found it necessary to rely on the help and goodness of others? We are all broken to some degree, and we all need the help of others to help us heal. The feeling of being exposed makes us mentally and emotionally vulnerable, but it is when we are open to others that we can both share in their journey and they can share in ours. It's a paradox, but being exposed makes us stronger if we allow it to.

Place your loved ones at the top of your to-do list; make them priority number 1. To thrive in brokenness, you need an army. In times of intense struggle remember who you are and rely on your army, God, and those people God sends to you.

CHAPTER 7

GLIMPSES

Matt is a true example of faith in the storm and God is exemplified in him, even in his lowest moments.

– Bobbye Jean Manzari

I magine waking up surrounded by various shades of white in a clean and sterile environment. You are cold, bewildered, and completely unable to move. Now take a moment and stick your fingers in your ears. What do you hear? That is what I heard and felt when I woke up. All I could do was move my eyes around the room. Everything was fuzzy. I could make out images of people and lights, but they had some sort of gel over my eyes so I could not see anything very clearly. There was a faint beeping in the background coming from the monitors behind me. Tubes were coming out from everywhere I could see. An IV line in my arm, oxygen tubes in my nose, and more tubes everywhere it seemed possible. My head, neck, arms, chest, and thighs were concealed by one huge white bandage. Every visible part of my body looked like a cartoon version of a mummy. Only this was not fake; it was real.

It felt like I was dreaming. You know that feeling you get when you are dreaming and you try to run but you cannot? Or you wake up, but feel like you are still dreaming and you do not know where you are? That is what it was like for me. I was lying there trying to figure it all out. Then I was able to focus on one person in the room, a man. He was dressed in all white, and I could hear his voice.

"Matt, you are in the ICU. You have been electrocuted."

He was very straightforward. I was nearing the end of my life and with all of the skin basically melted off my chest, sternum, and arms, it was not likely I would make it through the night. I would go septic and infection would go to my heart. His prognosis for me was about four to six hours. It was bad. He told me if I had any last remarks I wanted to say to my family then I should probably tell them. He told me to go ahead and get a living will if I did not already have one. Not the best of news. I basically had to prepare to die. How do you do that? I do not remember much more of this day. It was day three after the accident, and I faded back into unconsciousness. However, I lived through that night. My body was not ready to give up.

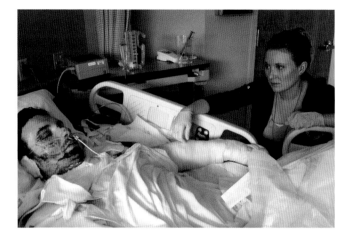

Bobbye Jean was a constant presence.

There was extensive damage to my body, which would require a lot of healing. At best, the situation was bleak. The doctors were trying to prepare my family for the worst. They assumed my brain was too damaged for a full recovery, and with my chest being open, they were sure my heart had to be damaged as well. Their combined knowledge and experience suggested that infection would take over and my kidneys would shut down. There did not appear to be much hope.

My family could not comprehend what they were seeing either. My feet were the only thing they could touch. They struggled to keep the faith that behind all the bandages and tubes I was still me. Bobbye Jean was trying to be a pillar of strength for me and everyone else but she was dealing with horrible haunting flashbacks from the scene of the accident. If that was not enough to process, the doctors were telling my family they had to remove my arms. Both of my arms all the way to the shoulder. Doing so was the only way to help keep me alive. With no circulation in either arm, the potential for infection was almost guaranteed. Just one damaged muscle is toxic enough to shut down the kidneys and result in heart failure. Both of my arms were damaged. I was like a ticking time bomb. The surgery appointment to remove my arms was set for the next morning. Everyone's nerves were on edge.

My family fought to the end with the doctors about pushing the surgery back. Eventually, the head surgeon called one of their best orthopedic surgeons at home and asked him to come in. He performed a drastic procedure called Fasciotomy. It was a surgical procedure where the fascia is cut to relieve tension or pressure commonly to treat the resulting loss of circulation to an area of tissue or muscle. My arms were turning black due to the loss of circulation and this was a last-ditch effort to save my arms. I am sure I no longer have any of my original blood left in my body. The average human body holds eight to nine units (a unit is about the same as a pint) of blood and I am sure they have used three times that amount between this procedure and other surgeries I underwent. Amazingly, the swelling went down, and it was not necessary to remove my arms. My arms were saved. This was just one of the many miracles that would continue to happen.

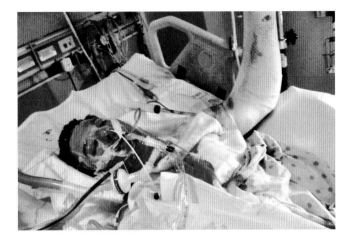

After the procedure to save my arms.

I was heavily medicated and faded in and out of consciousness over the next two weeks. During this time, I had several surgeries to continue removing the dying tissue and muscle to prevent me from becoming septic. Most burn victims die from the infection that sets in instead of the actual burns themselves. I do have brief glimpses of memories from this time but still was not fully aware of my condition. At one point I was told I used an alphabet board to communicate. By week two, I was actively communicating. This eased my family's minds about brain damage. Even though my communications probably did not make much sense due to the medication, I was still in there and able to communicate with them. Within two months of the accident, I was conscious and aware enough to begin to understand the severity of the situation. I knew I was in the hospital; I just did not realize how much time had passed.

My next real memory was talking to everybody and asking if they were going to keep me overnight. In my mind, I had been coming down for a water break and was now in the hospital. It felt like the same day to me. After realizing it had been longer, I started asking if I would be able to able to go on the trip to Alaska I had planned with my friend Will. Then I learned the trip had happened a couple of weeks before. My friend, Seth, had gone for me and had already come back home. I just could not wrap my head around how much time had passed. It did not seem possible that I had missed two months of my life.

At that moment all I could say was,
"Am I going to die?"

My family tried to explain everything that had happened to me. I only remember trying to understand how severe my condition really was, but I could not wrap my head around it. I recall them trying to describe to me what was under all the bandages. The fact that my chest was completely compromised. I did not understand exactly what that meant. They told me that my skin had actually melted off. It was gone. At that moment all I could say was, "Am I going to die?" All they could say was, "We do not know." At one moment, it seemed life was coming together; in another moment, it seemed life had just collapsed again.

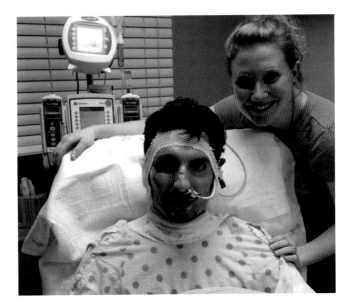

I was awake but still confused about all that had just happened.

What do you do when you wake up to an entirely different, almost unrecognizable version of yourself? What do you do when life as you know it not only shifts but completely changes in a way you least expect?

This might be the end of my life. All of the dreams I had for my life, everything I had imagined for myself, might actually not happen. For most of my life, I was a professional athlete. Would I ever be on the water again? My amazing wife was three, almost four months pregnant. We were parents to be. Would I ever get to meet our child? Would I ever get to hold our baby in my arms or stand beside my wife as our new baby came into the world? If I survived, how capable would I be as a husband and a father?

This is what happens when you are faced with death. You start to question everything you ever did. You arrive at an internal place where you mourn your whole life. Glimpses of your past, your childhood, everything that led up to this moment, arise. All the time you spent preparing for moments that would never happen…. Glimpses of how you thought you would experience having a family. You thought you would see the northern lights or learn to skydive… whatever dreams you anticipated.

Then you must come to a place where you are at peace with all you did not do. It is just like losing a loved one. You mourn, but eventually you have to accept it. Initially, you may find yourself denying the situation and wanting to fight, but there is also a level of acceptance. You have these waves of emotions where you believe that your life does not end here, as this was not your plan for your life. Then you come to the realization that things have changed indefinitely, and you have to be okay with it. This is not an easy thing to do.

Here I gathered strength from the experience of my first accident. I had seen God work, and I knew He could again. I did not have control over the fact that my life may be ending, but I had control over my attitude. I had control over how I could live out my remaining time. I did not want to spend my last days crying or mourning. I wanted to be smiling, giving my family the best of me while I was still here. With each day that passed and each surgery I survived, I began to see glimpses of hope. Hope that I might walk out of this storm. My attitude to fight grew with each passing day. I was going to make it out. I was going to see the birth of my child. I was going to thrive. I was going to remember who I was.

The joy of this little life growing kept me fighting.

....

GLIMPSES REFLECTION

Reflect on a time of change in your life, a time when you had to decide to either give up or fight. What compelled you to fight? How did God help you through the most difficult days?

When encountering difficult or hurtful circumstances, emotions change quickly. It is the mindset with which you approach the future that determines the outcome. Trusting in God and believing in His love for you is the anchor needed during times of hurt and His presence is your hope.

CHAPTER 8

LIMITS

Every day I was pushed beyond my limits.

– Matt Manzari

What are our limits? Do we really know how far we can be pushed? At this point in my recovery, I was fully aware and could feel the pain associated with my situation. I had to answer the question, "Do you want to get well?" I know that is a very strange question. You are probably thinking, "Who would not want to get well?" Most people want to be well, but do not want to put in the work to get better. It takes action on our part and a different mindset. When things are tough, we usually want to retreat as that is the easier course of action.

There is an interesting story on this matter in Sripture. In John 5:1-18 we see a man lying on the ground. Jesus walks up to him and asks, "Do you want to get well?" The man responds by explaining all of the reasons why he could not. As the story is told, there was a pool of water that when the waters stirred, the first person in the water would be healed. The man starts out by telling Jesus that there was no one to take him to the water. Then the next excuse, everyone beats me there. The question was, "Do you want to get well?" This seems like such an obvious question, but it is not. If this man gets well, he has to pay taxes, he has to get a job, and he will also have lots of other responsibilities. It requires action to be well. It would change his lifestyle. Did he really want to do that?

It is the same question for us. We say we want to get well, but do we? We have all heard people that say, "Well you know how I am; I am just always stressed." They want to change, but they do not want to put in the work to move forward. They have made it part of their identity, just like the man in the story. His illness was part of his identity. We have to decide every day to get up and face whatever challenge comes our way. When you are hurt or sick, you are in a war. To win the war, there are daily battles that have to be conquered. My electrocution accident was my war. One of the major battles I had to face was wound dressing changes and scrubbings.

Our skin is the first line of defense against infection. The slightest scratch or unseen mark that breaks the skin can increase the chances of infection creeping into our body. What do you think my chances were? I was lying in a hospital bed with the skin missing from my chest and arms. To say I was at risk for infection is an extreme understatement, hence the need for dressing changes. This meant that every twenty-four hours, I had a new battle to face. My wound dressings had to be taken off, cleaned, and changed. That probably sounds like a simple task, but this was an intense procedure that had to be performed every day.

I do not remember much about my wound scrubbing in the beginning because I was often sedated. Each wound scrubbing took about two or three hours. During the long procedure, I was not cognitively aware of what was happening, but I still felt pain enough, which caused me to scream. Thank goodness for the sedation. When they finished the scrubbing, they would slowly stop the flow of the medication into my IV line, and I would come out of it completely unaware of the fact that a wound scrubbing took place.

One of my champions from this time was my dad. He made the decision to be in the room with me for every dressing change. I know it could not have been easy for him to watch his child lie there in agony. My rib cage, my sternum, and my clavicle were all visible, being there was no tissue or muscle to cover them up. He wanted to spare my wife and mom from having to watch me suffer in that way. He chose to bear that burden instead of them. I will be forever grateful to him.

As a dad, you are watching your son be tortured for two hours, knowing it will all happen again in six hours. You hear

those screams and there is nothing you can do for him.
–Darren Manzari

There was a time during my recovery when they had to start reducing the amount of sedation they could use. I became very aware during this time and started remembering more and more of the wound scrubbings. One of the wound scrubbings during this time was very traumatic for me. They moved me into the room and were getting things ready when, just before they started the medicine, I caught a glimpse of my arm for the very first time. It was only a small area of my forearm, but all I could see was bone and what I thought were veins. There was such a contrast between the healthy skin and the injured part. There was hair and skin that looked perfectly normal and then nothing that resembled an arm. As they put me under for the procedure, my arm was the last image in my brain. Upon waking from these procedures my memory was usually fuzzy or nonexistent. Today it was perfectly clear. As I looked at my bandaged arm all I could see was the image I fell asleep to, an unrecognizable arm. What would I find under the rest of my bandages? I could not even imagine how anyone could survive this. How was I going to? The image of my arm caused nightmares for some time, even after I was home.

The whole recovery process was stressful and unbearable at times. There is one "worst day ever" that I recall. My legs had been used as donor sites for skin grafts two weeks before this day. My wounds should have been healed in that time, but I was still in so much pain. On this particular day, the nurses were unable to remove the dressings from my legs. It was almost as if someone had taken super glue and used it to attach my dressings to my body. They put me in a waterproof mattress, and for hours, poured gallons of saline over my legs while I attempted to pull the dressing off my leg. I sat in a shallow bathtub of blood and saline for hours. It was so much work to make such little progress or gain any ground. I remember the two nurses pouring a whole gallon of saline on my leg and I would just scream as loud as I could as I tried to pull back the bandage. I felt like I was gaining ground until I looked down and realized I had only pulled less than a centimeter back. The entire process felt like I was pulling my own skin off piece by piece. It took an hour to do one thigh, and at the end of my first leg, I was so defeated and in so much physical pain that I could not imagine pulling the dressing of off my other thigh. It was like my legs were on fire.

I was sitting in a literal pool of my own blood mixed with saline wanting to quit but knowing the dressing from the other leg had to be taken off as well. I so desperately wanted to stop. I wanted the agony to stop. I kept hoping the pain would knock me out, but it never did. Nothing could numb the torment. No one, not even my loved ones, could pull me from the fact the dressing had to be removed from the other leg. My family begged for me to be sedated but this was one of those times they could not sedate me. I can recall feeling almost entirely hopeless. Nothing could fix it. Even if I wanted to run from it there was no way I could. This was one of the toughest obstacles I had to overcome, one of the many. Here at this moment is where I realized that getting well was and is a deliberate choice.

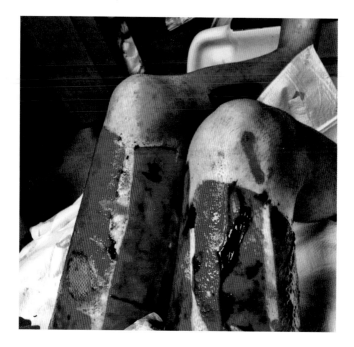

Skin grafts from my legs.

Many of you might understand getting stretched to the end of your limits. You may be in so much pain that every little thing keeps adding up until you feel you might break. Little things that you usually would not care about now seem unbearable.

Sometimes we resist the path we are on and try to stay in control. Just like a kid who refuses to get ready for school. They really do not have a choice, but they dig in their heels thinking it will make a difference. I was so over being poked and prodded and being in pain. I remember one incident when they were trying to get the central line to an artery in my heart. The doctor said if he gets it right, it will only hurt for a second. Well, he missed five times. I should have been put under for the procedure, but I had been under so many times that they felt it was better for me to just "suck it up" and move through it. I had been pushed to my limit again. The doctor stopped because he could not continue to see me in so much pain. He scheduled to have me sedated. He was pushed to his limit as well. Being able to see his emotion validated mine. It was hard on me, but for the first time, I realized how hard it was for those around me having to watch me suffer.

Realizing this helped me to continue fighting the battles to succeed in winning this war. I had to keep pushing my limits and working hard to get well. Every day I had to find the positive for that day. My recovery consisted of extreme highs and lows intertwined together. There are two days I remember very well as highs. One was when my wife and therapist snuck me outside for the first time. Just feeling the wind hit my legs made me feel human again. The other was our gender reveal they did with a popsicle. I cannot even begin to explain the joy inside me when I saw a blue popsicle.

It reminded me to fight even harder so I could help raise my son. Sometimes we just have to keep focused on the positive of every situation. It is there, even if it is hard to see at times. It is all about our choices.

While you may or may not have experienced extreme physical pain, each one of us can relate to suffering and hurt. Whether the pain is physical, emotional, or both does not matter. What matters is this: you need community to heal.

It takes an army to win a war, and we are all in a war of some sort. We all need others, family, friends, loved ones, even strangers to help fight our battles. Today I encourage you to reach out to others and either ask for help if you need it or be a soldier in someone else's army, a soldier for someone you know is hurting.

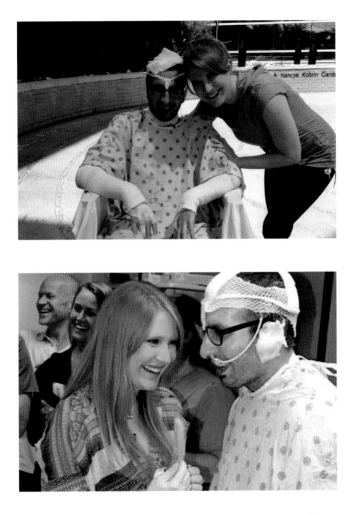

Both of these days were amazing! Feeling the wind on my legs and learning I was having a boy!

Getting well comes with an ultimatum:
Get well and thrive, or retreat and give up.

Getting well comes with an ultimatum: Get well and thrive, or retreat and give up. I chose to get well and on September 13, 2014, just eighty days after they said I would not live through this accident, I left the hospital. I still have challenges to overcome, but I am choosing to get well. I believe the plans for my life are far more significant than the burn scars on my skin and I am learning to thrive in spite of those scars. You can make the same choice in your life. You can overcome your struggles. Will you push beyond your limits and thrive?

Time to go home!

LIMITS REFLECTION

When were you stretched beyond your limits and felt that you might break? Did you try to remain in control of an uncontrollable situation? How did you arrive at the decision to fight, and what was the outcome?

We all have challenges to overcome. Some of us have physical struggles, some mental, and some of us endure both. What we all have in common is that we can all push beyond our limits and thrive. Daily, we can intentionally love the person we are and the life we live now.

I challenge you to push beyond your limits every day and thrive!

CHAPTER 9

HUMBLED

Humility isn't thinking less of yourself, but
thinking of yourself less.

– C.S. Lewis

Y ou learn the value of humility when faced with the fact you cannot walk, go to the bathroom, or get a shower without help. Both of my accidents positioned me in very vulnerable places. My electrocution accident was definitely a much longer hospital stay and re- covery period. I went from the role of husband and future father to a man needing assistance with everything. I could not even open a water bottle by myself. As a husband, I was supposed to be my wife's and children's provider and pro- tector. I was struggling physically as well as mentally at this time. Not being able to fulfill the head of my household role throughout the recovery process took an emotional toll on me.

Sometimes the emotional struggle is harder to deal with than the physical one. You start to feel like such a burden when you cannot pull your own weight. This point in time is where I learned one of the biggest lessons of this entire experience. We are never above taking someone else's help or advice. We can always use some type of assistance and we can always learn something from someone else. In the hospital, any pride I ever felt in myself had been stripped away. I was unable to do the most personal things for myself. It was like being a child all over again. I went from one minute being able to manage and handle things by myself to continually needing someone around me at all times. I felt like a complete burden no matter how many times my family assured me I was not.

Humility helps to build our character, and it is a necessary part of growing us as a person.

Humility helps to build our character, and it is a necessary part of growing us as a person. It shows the value of community and it magnifies Christ's ability to do crazy, wondrous things in our lives. My accidents made me utterly dependent on the help and support of others. I had to lean on Christ and trust He would do what He was infinitely capable of doing. I had to trust God would pull through, and I promise you, He has pulled through for me every time without fail. In every situation I could see God working. He was walking with me through the challenges. It may not have been in my timing or what I thought I needed, but it all worked out for the best in the end.

Our culture teaches us that for a man to be the head of the household, he has to be tough. Taking any type of help from anyone basically means we, as men, are weak. This is also an area where pride comes in. Think about it, how often do we refuse to accept help, even when we know we will not be judged? Pride is the reason men do not ask for directions even when they know they are lost. This is also true of single parents. They tend to feel like failures if they have to ask for help. Needing help is not a bad thing. We are created to live and thrive as part of a community. We are designed to help and to need each other.

This lesson was tough for me to learn. Even though I knew I needed help, I still felt like a burden. My family and friends were taking huge breaks out of their lives for me. The hospital room was always full of visitors. While I was excited to see them, I also knew they were making enormous sacrifices. The unselfishness and kindness of others is not always the world's most natural thing to accept. If we think about it, not wanting to receive help is such a selfish thing. So often, we just want to prove ourselves to others. We want others to think we are strong even when we are falling apart and are in desperate need of help. We want them to believe we are in control and that we can do it all on our own. Right under the surface we are falling apart and are too stubborn to ask for help. We have all been there.

Do you remember a time when you were desperate but too afraid to let others know you needed help? How did you feel when someone stepped up for you? Maybe you are a single parent who just needs a break. Maybe you have been battling a mental or physical illness on your own. Regardless of what it is, I am here to say it is time to ask for and accept help.

I came to a point in my recovery where I let go of my selfish thoughts and mentally allowed myself to be helped. I really had no other options. It was not like I could refuse the help and care of the doctors and nurses. I knew that everyone just wanted the best for me and wanted me well. I was grateful for all the help I had, and it taught me to be humble. It taught me how to accept help without letting my pride get in the way. I am so appreciative of the support I had. Going through everything I did has enabled me to be able to recognize desperation in others. It now gives me the opportunity to help others in some way. I could never repay all the help I received, but I can at least try to pay it forward.

Bobbye Jean and I have had many opportunities to give

our support to other families going through tragedies. One of the saddest things we have witnessed is watching some of those families being ripped apart by the stress. During a stressful time, families will either grow closer together or they will fall apart. It takes effort on everyone's part to stay together. I am sure you have seen this as well. A couple loses a child and they start the blame game with each other, causing the marriage to fall apart. Or a family member is diagnosed with a terminal illness. One of the spouses is so busy tending to the family member that the other one feels neglected. Maybe an affair happens. I know these are harsh examples, but they happen all the time.

Realizing this, I have to tell you my greatest hero throughout this healing process has been Bobbye Jean. Her *What to Expect When You Are Expecting* book did not have a chapter on your husband almost dying while you are pregnant. Any thoughts of leaving me during this time never entered her mind, even when they said the brain damage would be severe. As a matter of fact, she envisioned herself an eighty-year-old woman sitting on the porch feeding me soup and telling me about her day. With the hope that just a little bit of me was still there. Bobbye Jean has been by my side through every surgery. She is the true hero in my story. She is a partner who has a servant's heart and takes her marriage vows seriously.

Brokenhearted is exactly how I felt. God was close to me and kept me from being crushed by the weight of this trial.
–Bobbye Jean Manzari

When hard times come, or we feel our integrity has been challenged, we have one of two choices to make: be bitter or be better. I was tested in this way while in the hospital. I had to decide for myself. Every day, someone on this planet is offered an opportunity and a challenge. Every day, a person has to decide whether or not they will choose to be better or stay bitter. Tragedy strikes and tragedy hurts deeply, but nothing in this life is ever meant to have a grip so tight it defeats us for years on end. Yet, this reality does not mean we are not allowed to grieve. This does not mean our pain is meaningless and does not matter. What it does mean, though, is that you are made for so much more than defeat and bitterness regardless of the circumstances.

We often use pain and suffering interchangeably. They are different though. Pain is caused by situations that happen in our lives and suffering is something that we choose. It is all about our attitude through the pain. I am not saying that pain is not real or that you should just put a fake smile on and be strong. But we can come to a place where we say that if God never did another thing for us, we would still owe Him the rest of our life. Sometimes we have to reach deep within and find that level of humble courage.

The world shows us that courage means someone is able to overcome the emotional effects of a situation and move forward. This may make the person with courage appear to be removed or indifferent. You know that cool guy at the end of the movie who is stone-faced? I would rather look at Jesus's example. He was the ultimate man of courage. He was here for a very specific purpose, but still had emotions. One of the most powerful verses in the Bible is John 11:35, "Jesus wept." In this story, Mary and Martha had reached out to Jesus to come heal their sick brother. When He shows up a few days later, Lazarus was already dead. Mary and Martha were crushed and angry that Jesus had shown up too late. At this moment Jesus knew what He was going to do. He knew Lazarus would be resurrected and everyone would become joyful again. Feeling the weight of the pain around Jesus brought compassion for those hurting, causing Him to weep. Just because Jesus showed some emotion, it did not change His course.

Courage is not ignoring the pain, but it is trusting the truth and staying the course. It is saying that even though this hurts, it is not time to rethink your faith. Though your marriage is in a difficult place, it does not mean that you are broken and incapable of being in a relationship. Things happen to us, but they do not need to break us. They can and should strengthen us.

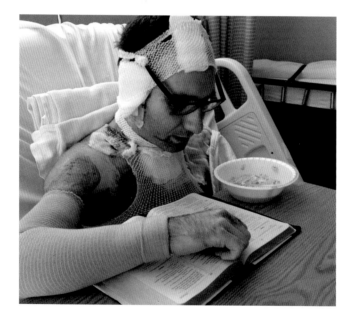

I found comfort in studying my Bible.

I get many questions about my recovery process. They all wonder how I handle not being able to do the things I used to. My answer is always the same. I am different in many ways from who I was before my accidents. I might be young and a person my age should not have to experience as much physical pain as I have, but I've accepted that I will never be who I was.

We will never be who we once were, for better or for worse. No matter how hard we try to cling to the past, life still moves forward. I may not be able to do everything I used to do as well as I once did, but I am still alive and can still continue growing. I just have to remain humble and continue learning how to thrive through the tragedies of life. I had to remember who I was.

....

HUMBLED REFLECTION

Reflect on a time when you really needed help but were afraid to ask for it. How did you feel when someone stepped up to help you?

Being humble builds character. When have you had to humble yourself and ask for help from others? What did you learn about community through the process?

If asking for help is difficult for you, consider how you might allow others to see your needs and respond. Lifelong bonds are created through helping one another.

CHAPTER 10

ILLUSIONS

A good way to stop growth is to wait for a clear picture.

– Matt Manzari

During my journey, I have met people from all walks of life—young and old, rich and poor, with different situations and struggles. The majority of them tend to use similar phrases to describe their lives such as, "I am getting by," "I am surviving," or "We are making ends meet." I am sure you have heard these or even spoken them yourself at some point in your life. Are these neutral phrases really okay? Just because they are common, does not mean they are harmless. Yet each time we hear or say them, they become validated in our minds. Then we start to justify them and thus start believing we have no hope. These phrases do not build us up; they only tear us down. It amazes me how normalized these negative thoughts have become in our society. People allow these thoughts to consume them for months or even years. How sad is it to lose such valuable time stuck in such a negative position and outlook? This can easily happen in relationships, jobs, marriages, and many other areas of our life where we struggle. And when we allow our mindset to be negative it is hard to persevere through our struggles.

Have you ever found yourself looking at your life through a neutral lens? You know the one that makes you feel like you are not moving forward? I believe we all have at one time or another. At some point in our lives, we have found ourselves feeling stagnant. Are we ever really stationary? How can we have the illusion of being neutral when we live in an ever-changing world? Our social environment, our government, our tax system, our economy, and many other issues the world faces are ever-changing. In a world that is so volatile and uncertain, it would be crazy to believe that we are the one constant that never changes. The truth is, there is no such thing as remaining neutral or "getting by." We are always moving. We are either growing or we are choosing to be dying.

When we are in the middle of a battle, we want to feel strong. I think we really want to believe in the illusion that we are in control. We do not want people to think we are weak or seeking too much attention, so we tell them everything is okay. The very foundations of our lives may be falling apart, but we play the part of having everything together. I believe we do this because it is easier to hide behind our illusions. There is no neutral position here and what eventually happens is that we end up leaning toward a negative perspective of our lives. We have to admit we are changing regardless of if we want to believe it or not.

If you are reading this book inside your home, a coffee shop, the break room at work, or any other location, I want you to look around for a second. Look at the scenery—the walls, look at the paint, the windows, and the floors. Do you notice anything out of the ordinary? Probably not. However, the reality is that there might be many things wrong with the building or location you are in that remain hidden. If you were to totally abandon the building or location you are in now and return twenty years from now, chances are that you would hardly recognize it. Think about all the dust that would have collected. There might even be bugs crawling around. Maybe the roof would be leaking, causing mold to grow. The paint may be faded and chipped. Without constant renovations, maintenance, and upkeep the building will certainly weather and fall apart. The process is much too slow for us to see though. This same metaphor applies to our lives.

We often go through life with a "getting by" mindset. We do the bare minimum required to get by because that is all that is needed. But then, twenty years later we may look in the mirror and not recognize the person looking back at us. We are a totally different person than we had hoped to be and have no idea how we ended up here. We look back at the ambitious child we once were, full of dreams, goals, and visions of who we were going to be. Now we are not even the spouse, friend, parent, or the employee/employer that we thought we would be. The result of a series of countless small compromises of the standard we set for our lives can be devastating. These compromises are compounded over days, weeks, months, and years, and they change who we are in a big way. If we allow it, we will also deteriorate slowly over time just like the building.

We have to choose to continually renovate and grow in our lives. We have to allow ourselves to grow and change through our experiences and struggles. If we do not take that first step toward growth, we will end up in a situation where we are looking in the mirror and wondering who we are or what we have become. The second thing we must do is learn to focus on others. I believe focusing on others can be a huge step toward a better attitude in our own lives. Our world may teach us that it is all about "me," but this attitude will leave us lonely. We may reach the top of the mountain, but it is lonely and there is no oxygen at the top. We are designed to function as a member of a community, and as such, we will always have help and also be in a position to help others, which greatly enriches our lives.

We always need to be content with what we have, but never with who we are.

– Matt Manzari

Contentment is a tricky thing. We are told to be content with our lives and material things we own, as we are bombarded with the next best thing. Every commercial talks about something new you need or how to change something on your body. I believe we need to be content with what we have but not with who we are. Let me explain. We should be thankful for what we have in life. Not everyone has the best of the best but we can still find joy and contentment with where we are. As far as who we are, we should want to grow more every day. Whether Bobbye Jean and I were living in our tiny apartment on the other side of town or the beautiful house we live in now on the lake, I have always been content with what I have in life. I have not been content with who I am though. I am constantly focused on how I can be better. What I have learned is that helping others can supply that contentment. I end up getting what I want when I help others. Of course, this is never my motivation. I know the truth is that as I focus more on others, my own success comes as a result of that. As long as I am pouring myself into others, I am satisfied. Hence, I am growing more and more. We can always find joy and contentment in whatever circumstance we may be in. It is a challenge to find that mindset but it is fulfilling when you do.

As we are pouring into others we have to remember to take care of ourselves. Think about a reservoir. Maybe you are picturing a large tank filled with water. If you throw a bucket of water out of it every hour, eventually the tank will be empty. We can give and give to others but we will eventually become empty. Do you know someone who gave until they completely fell apart? Maybe it was you. We have to continually refill our tanks; take some time to recharge. I am one of those people who enjoys giving to others. I find great joy in helping someone who is struggling. My tank would eventually become empty if I did not take some downtime with my family to fill my tank back up. Take a moment to do a check on your tank. Do you need to fill it back up?

Finding joy by helping others.

I enjoy talking to people during my travels and asking them what is on their bucket list. Sometimes I am able to help that person. One time I was able to take a kid from a coffee shop skydiving. He will remember that event. You may be thinking I cannot help anyone. I can barely pay my own bills. Sometimes it is just our time that is required.

Maybe that person only needs someone to listen to them.

Every day I try to answer the following questions: Am I living actively or passively? Every day I should be actively looking at who I might meet that day. Can I have an impact on another person's life? How am I going to grow today? When we live passively, we go through the day completing task after task, with the idea that there is never enough time to do anything but get by. Living this way is merely allowing life to push you around, instead of you pushing back at life. We are never promised life would be easy. We have to embrace the difficulties and allow them to help us grow. A neutral position in life is only an illusion. Remember who you are.

....

ILLUSIONS REFLECTION

When have you been in a "getting by" mindset? Are you in one now? If so, it is time to move forward. It is time to change gears from neutral to drive.

Growth is a mindset too. To change from a "getting by" to a "growth" mindset, follow my example and ask yourself each day if you are living actively or passively and consider how you can grow each day. Remember that the key to growth is helping others, so make a commitment to help someone each time you can. Whether you help by offering a listening ear, running an errand, or any other helpful action, by helping another, you grow personally.

CHAPTER 11

UNFAIR

At least if I died, I died me.

– Matt Manzari

I saw the perfect example of how we react when tragedy strikes by watching my son one day. We were in the kitchen, and my son had his pacifier in his mouth. I do not know if you have seen the devastation that takes place when a "binky" falls out of a baby's mouth, but it is life changing. His or her whole world comes to an end. Judging by his attitude, I am pretty sure if he could talk he would have said, "Why am I even here? What is the point of life after this? I cannot go on."

We adults look down like, "Little dude, your world is not over. The binky is not gone forever; it is actually clipped to your shirt. Somebody needs to take it down like ten thousand notches because we have overcome the binky issue."

Then, as we get a little older and our heart is broken for the first time, it feels like our world is shattered. Our friends and parents cannot fix it. But sure enough, as time passes, everything is okay. Then we grow up, and we forget we are that way. We lose a job or a loved one; we are burnt, injured, or end up in a wheelchair, and once again our world comes crashing down. I picture God looking down at us seeing our limited minds devastated once again saying, "Little dude, I have overcome the binky issue. I have overcome the grave. What are a few years of living in a broken, burnt body when you are on the verge of eternity in a perfect one?"

For our light and momentary troubles are achieving for us an eternal glory that far outweighs them all.
–2 Corinthians 4:17 NIV

Is life unfair? Sure it is. That is what we have been told our entire lives. Do you remember being a teenager and something did not go your way? What would your parents say? "Sorry, life is not fair." Is it really a surprise that we have chosen that mindset? I believe because of statements like this, we have slid down the slippery slope of negative thinking. So many of us feel that we do not get what we deserve and that we are entitled to a better life. But why is that? What are those thoughts based on? Why do you think you deserve more than what you have? Thinking this way may be the norm, but just because most people feel this way does not mean it is right. So why do so many people feel this way? Do they know some law of nature that I have never heard of that gives them validation for their thoughts? Have they read something in the Bible that says we deserve this or that? I have not read anything like that, nor do I believe that we have any basis for this mindset. What I have come to believe is that we actually deserve for things to be much harder than they are.

Everyone wants things to be fair. Even as far back as when we were kids, and we were splitting a candy bar with our sibling. We had to make sure that each piece was the same size before we ate ours. We wanted things to be fair. But what does fair or unfair really mean in our lives? It is a perspective and mindset. We choose what we think is fair or unfair based on what we believe to be true.

We need to start focusing on the fact that every day is a gift and tomorrow is never promised.

I believe fair is when something that should happen, happens. I believe that unfair is when something that we don't think is fair, happens. If you touch the stove while it is on, what happens? You get burned. Do you blame God or life for being unfair because you touched a hot stove? No, you blame yourself because you touched the hot stove and you knew the consequences. I know it is hard to be struggling, but our mindset needs to be different in that struggle. We need to realize that we do not deserve anything and nobody owes us anything. We do not deserve to live in homes with air conditioning while most of the world lives in homes without a floor. We need to start focusing on the fact that every day is a gift and tomorrow is never promised.

Why is it that I survived? The best doctors in Central Florida at the only Level 1 trauma center, who are rarely wrong, said, "Not if, but when your kidneys fail." They were sure I had brain damage and heart damage. They were confident my arms were going to be removed. They were certain they were doing their job to keep me comfortable until I died.

Why were the best doctors wrong again and again? I am convinced it is because we serve an unfair God, who, for an unmerited reason, steps into this world and says, "This is still My world; these are still My people, and I will have the last say." This is the God I serve. One who has given me everything through His Word. He has given me all the tools I need to lay my challenges at the cross, and He offers the same thing to all who choose to believe in Him.

I am asked these questions all the time:

"Do you ever ask why?"

"Why if you serve this 'good God' did this happen?"

And, "Are you angry?"

I think these are all questions that people ask when they are faced with a tragedy. We all wonder why something happens, especially if it appears to be a negative or bad situation. This is how I usually answer those questions. "God has already given me the world. He has already given me an eternity. So, if my burden is the reality I am going to live in pain the rest of my life or even die tomorrow, He does not owe it to me to change it. Regardless, this situation might have been intended to harm me."

However, as it says in Genesis 50:20, "As for you, you meant evil against me, but God meant it for good" (ESV). God steps in to make good come out of the bad. I think God's plan was for me to use my platform as an action sports athlete and reach the youth. After my accidents, He then said, "If you trust Me with this situation, I can take this farther than you can ever imagine. I will make more good come out of this than bad ever can." I truly believe God can use any tragedy for His glory.

Being burned and having my body broken and disfigured did not in any way seem light and momentary. It was hard to see past the next hour or even the next few minutes, let alone try to think about eternity. Now that I am on the other side, I can see the outcome of those troubles. It is much easier to see how small, in the grand scheme of things, those troubles and these next fifty to sixty, if not more, years are. In light of eternity, my life here on earth pales in comparison.

I decided that to be miserable, sad, and depressed all the time was not going to make me any less electrocuted. I could not change the fact I was going to be in pain or possibly even die. However, I could make the decision to have a good attitude, regardless of the situation. I could sulk and be sad, or I could pour every last bit of who I was into my family and friends. I could let them know how much I loved them and how much they meant to me every day. I could choose to pour hope and value into them. At least if I died, I died me. I would go out on top, letting my friends and family know there is more to this life than what we see. I would be remembered for leaving a character-based legacy about who I was.

Selfishly, I wanted to be there the day my son was born. I wanted to stand by my wife's side and hold our little boy. This was not a promise I was given. I did not deserve to be there. I was not owed the opportunity. How could I ask somebody for something who had already given me everything? The Bible tells us in John 16:33, "In this world, you will have trouble. But take heart! I have overcome the world" (NIV). It is hard to see beyond the fifty to one hundred years we have here on earth. Sometimes it is a struggle to see beyond the next month, week, day, or even the next hour. It is especially difficult when you are walking through a painful situation. SPOILER ALERT: GOD wins! And we get eternity.

We do not need to live in fear or mourn our situation.

How did I get through every day of my struggle toward recovery? I made small reachable goals. I can remember looking at the whiteboard beside my hospital bed and getting to see what the day would hold. My skin had been totally burned off, and they adhered a layer of Integra onto my body to cover the muscle tissue and bone in preparation for skin grafts. As they began the process of replacing my skin, I soon found out it was going to be a long and painful process. Excruciating, actually. Seeing the plans for the day on the little whiteboard next to my bed was basically like accepting the fact that I was about to be tortured. An upcoming surgery here, wound scrubbing there, and another surgery the next day, followed by more wound scrubbings and dressing changes.

Each morning I would look at the day, become totally overwhelmed and then say, "I cannot try right now to make it to tonight, but I can make it to eleven." Then I looked toward one that afternoon. The next thing I knew I was making it through full days, then full weeks, then full months, and then I was being discharged. Then, it was time for my son to be born. How amazing is that? God allowed me the opportunity to stand by my wife and watch my son come into this world.

It is okay to ask, "Why?" We just have to keep the big picture, the eternal perspective, in mind. We have to learn to thrive in the midst of the whys. How do we do that? By realizing where we are in life is a blessing. When we take charge of our mindset, we can begin to get the results that will put us in a more favorable situation. When we look past the reflection, we begin to see the real person and what we are capable of.

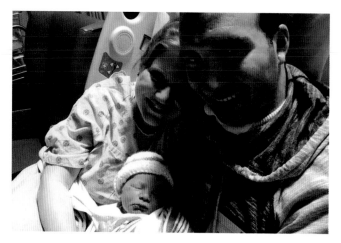

Meet Baby Justice.

....

UNFAIR REFLECTION

What circumstance or situation in your life was most unfair? Thinking back on that time, how did you move ahead or change direction from the hurt of injustice or personal injury and the emotion that comes with this mindset to deciding to try each and every day to continue living life to its fullest now? Even though the situation was not your fault, even though you probably felt and said, "It's not fair," what brought you out of the deep and into the realization that life was meant to be fully lived?

If you are at that crossroad now, are you ready to implement this mindset?

How do you keep the eternal picture in mind and thrive in the midst of the whys?

CHAPTER 12

REGARDLESS

Even if...God is still God.

– Bobbye Jean Manzari

When we face a challenge, there is a way to a solution that seems right to us, and then there is God's solution. If we try to do things our way, sometimes it means we have to face consequences and may find ourselves in a place that is more than we can handle. When we are tempted to lose hope, go down a dangerous road, or let our challenges defeat us, God is ready and waiting to take our hand and walk us through. And yes, He is always willing to help. We just have to ask Him. God never promised us a life of no pain, but He did promise us He would be there with us through the pain. In John 16:33, He tells us there will be suffering, but that we are to be at peace. He has overcome this world, and He is in control. When it is dark and we are afraid, we have to remember God is there. We need to have complete trust that through whatever situation or challenge we face, God will be there. He will be our constant. Even if the worst happens, God is still God.

We need to have complete trust that through whatever situation or challenge we face, God will be there.

When Bobbye Jean and I married, we had no idea what was in our future. We never could have imagined how much we would have to rely on God. We were just excited about what He was doing in our lives. Looking back today, we would not change any of it. We have seen God's goodness through all the challenges, and our marriage is stronger than we could have ever dreamed. Through our major challenges, I would hear people say, "You are so strong and courageous," or "I could never be that strong." I cannot count the times I heard, "God will never give you more than you can handle." I believe this is one of the most misquoted verses in the Bible. There is a lot that we cannot handle, but nothing that He cannot handle! The verse actually says, "He will not allow you to be tempted beyond what you can bear. But when you are tempted, he will also provide a way out so that you can endure it" (1 Cor. 10:13 NIV).

So, how do I appear courageous? Let us look at the definition of courageous. The Urban Dictionary defines a courageous person as one who is not deterred by danger or pain (www.urbandictionary.com/define.php?term=courageous). To have courage means to be brave. When I first read that, for a moment, it boosted my ego. As I really thought about it, though, I realized that it is a terrible definition of me. I am not brave. I was the little kid who was scared of the dark. If others see me as courageous, what are they seeing? As I moved through these challenges, I was not trying to put on a front or be fake; I was trying to be authentic. So I asked myself, what is it about the way I approach these situations that made it look like courageousness from the outside? I tend to believe it is because of another quality about me and that is "trust." Trust, according to Merriam-Webster Dictionary, is a firm belief in someone or something to be reliable or truthful (https://www.merriam-webster.com/dictionary/trust). I realized it is not that I was brave or courageous, as I had a lot of fears and doubts, but that I had a firm belief in someone or something. I had trust in God and His promises to be reliable and truthful, and His promises were bigger than all my fears and doubts.

I have heard many times that this all happened to me for a reason, yet I do not believe that we are part of a puppet show with God and Satan pulling all the strings. We all have free will and sometimes that means our choices lead to tragedies, like someone driving drunk and hurting themselves or others. Sometimes bad things happen simply because someone was not paying attention, and sometimes there is no real reason at all.

My electrocution accident happened because metal got too close to electricity. That is it. Science. One thing I have noticed is that if there is a loss, an injury, or tragedy of any kind in someone's life they become stuck and unable to move forward because they are constantly asking, "Why?"

How do we come to a point where we can stop asking why this has happened? Even if you feel justified in your pain or you feel like someone should be punished, staying stuck in the "why" will never change your situation. We need to start asking what is next. We may never fully understand our challenges, but we can continue growing, moving forward, and impacting those around us. We can come to a place where we are at peace, and we realize that our earthly life is not all we have. When we have a relationship with Jesus Christ, in the end, we will be in a place with no pain or suffering.

Blessed is the man who remains steadfast under trial, for when he has stood the test he will receive the crown of life, which God has promised to those who love him.
–James 1:12 ESV

We can all recognize that vulnerability, pain, and emotion are real and important parts of life. Having courage is not numbing the pain or acting like it is not there, but rather staying the course and trusting in the truth regardless of the pain. Writing this book has been very painful because there are memories that are still hard to revisit. My tears are all over the pages. That does not change the fact that I am still going to keep sharing my story and moving forward with what I know to be true. We can acknowledge what we have been through and that it hurts. Pain is an important part of life, and we are the people we are today because of it. We can turn our obstacles into opportunities, our bitter into better, and allow God to use our misery for His ministry. We just have to make the decision to either allow God to help or choose to let the struggles engulf us.

Rehab was difficult but so worth the challenge.

My therapy helper. Tala was my faithful friend through this process.

I have told you about our son who was born shortly after I left the hospital from my electrocution accident. Since then, God has blessed us with two more boys. Throughout the pregnancy with our third child, we faced struggles and challenges. At our twenty-weeks checkup, we were told something was wrong with the baby's heart. Specialist after specialist told us the same thing. The baby's heart was not developing properly. The right ventricle was completely solid in the ultrasound image. Being considered high risk, Bobbye Jean was at the doctor every Tuesday and Thursday for the remaining part of the pregnancy. After several appointments, the doctors informed us the baby would need a heart transplant if he survived to delivery. They also gave us the option of terminating the pregnancy. That was not an option for us. We knew it was going to be a struggle and his mortality rate was extremely high, but we continued praying for him to just make it to the delivery.

A couple of months before the due date, the doctors discovered an antibody in Bobbye Jean's blood that was preventing the baby's heart from developing. With an aggressive steroid approach, we started to see slow progress over time. The baby's heart was improving and the need for a transplant would not be immediate. When it came time for our child to be born, we were excited and nervous at the same time. Excited to meet our new family member and nervous about what he may have to endure medically. After delivery, they ran test after test and could not find anything wrong. No transplant would be needed at all. He was four weeks early and perfectly healthy, despite what we had been told during Bobbye Jean's pregnancy. That is the great God we serve. Watching my third son come into this world is just another story of God's goodness on display. The day of his birth was exactly four years to the day that I walked out of the hospital.

I love my crazy wonderful life!

We both handled the third pregnancy differently. I was convinced that everything was going to be fine and my mindset stayed there. Bobbye Jean went through all the emotions of possibly losing a child, even though that never happened. She still felt all those feelings. I am sure the emotions were different because she was the one actually carrying the child. It was very difficult for me to watch her experience such trauma. Maybe you have found yourself living through the emotions of something that you thought was going to happen but it never occurred.

Here is an example of what I am referring to. Maybe your boss yells at you one day and it rocks your world. You become convinced that you are going to get fired. You immediately start stressing about the bills that will not get paid. Where are you going to find another job? After a sleepless night, you go to work the next day and everything is fine. The boss apologizes, telling you he had a headache and was not feeling well. Then you take a deep breath and are thankful you do not have to start job hunting. Maybe you feel a little silly because you stressed over the possibility of being fired when the reality is it never happened.

I know these two examples are totally different spectrums. The emotions of possibly losing a child are more intense than possibly getting fired. But I am trying to get you to stop and think about how you react to circumstances that happen in your life. Do you jump to worst-case scenario every time? Do you allow the emotions to overtake you or do you try to look past the emotion and find a healthy way through the situation? Sometimes the worst will happen and you will have to deal with it. A lot of times, though, we put ourselves through unnecessary stress worrying about things that never happen.

> *I have been through some terrible things in my life, some of which actually happened.*
> –Mark Twain

I hope, as you have read my story, that you have accepted that everyone has challenges in life. Some are minor and some are major, but hopefully, some of the tools I developed to get through my own challenges can encourage you to take one more step toward victory. There is nothing special or unique about Bobbye Jean or me. We are regular people who faced some big challenges, just like you. We decided to choose a different attitude than the world offers, and as we faced challenges, we managed that decision. You will face challenges, and you can also decide to have a different attitude. Our focus now is to be a living testimony of how to thrive when the worst happens.

I speak all over the world to people from different backgrounds and cultures. No matter where I am, someone always asks, "If you could go back, would you change it?" This question has rocked my world more than any other, and I have thought about it over and over again. What would that moment be like—to talk to a younger version of myself? Everything in me would want to warn myself, so I could avoid all the pain. The answer, however, is no, I would not change it. If I could talk to my younger self, here is what I would say:

Matt, remember when you were younger and scared of the dark? You would sit in bed at night and think you heard a noise in the closet. The house would creak and you would think that something or someone was in the room or under the bed. Eventually, you would get so scared that you would jump out of bed and run to turn on the light. You would look around the room with your heart pounding and then realize the truth that nothing was there. You were safe, and everything was okay. You would calm down and realize that it was just your mind playing tricks. Then you would turn the light off and jump back into bed. Pretty quickly, as you sat in bed, your mind would start playing tricks again. While sitting in the darkness, you would forget the truth you had just learned in the light. You were safe, and everything was okay. You are fixing to go through some dark times, but I want you to face them with the light on, unafraid, because everything is going to be okay.

God has shown me more mercy and grace than I could have ever imagined. I have survived two near-death experiences, and I am still living a fulfilled life. Do I have scars and limitations? Of course I do. Do I live with daily pain, some days more so than others? Yes, but it has all become a part of who I am. I could wake up each day, feel sorry for myself, and wonder why this happened to me. Instead, I choose to have a better attitude. My hope is that someone sees me pushing through my pain and it brings even a small glimmer of hope to their struggle. It is not easy, and I do not know that it ever will be. I just have to constantly remind myself that my situation could be a lot worse and choose to focus on the gift of today. Because regardless of my circumstances, I have to remember that even if the worst happens, God is still God.

Enjoying life and continuing to fight through.

What will your choice be? Will you choose to face your struggles with a positive attitude, or will you choose to be bitter about your circumstances?

Are you going to live your life Beyond the Scars?

ENDNOTES

i.   Allers, Roger, Rob Minkoff, Don Hahn, Irene Mecchi, Jonathan Roberts, Linda Woolverton, Jonathan Taylor Thomas, et al. 2003. *The Lion King.*

ii. "Sir Roger Bannister: First person to run a mile in under four minutes dies at 88," BBC, accessed 3/19/2020, https://www.bbc.com/sport/athletics/43273249.